SCIENCE TIMELINES

THE DIGITAL AGE

1947-Present Day

By Charlie Samuels

W
FRANKLIN WATTS
LONDON • SYDNEY

First published in Great Britain in 2015 by
The Watts Publishing Group

Copyright © 2015 Brown Bear Books Ltd

For Brown Bear Books Ltd:
Editorial Director: Lindsey Lowe
Managing Editor: Tim Cooke
Children's Publisher: Anne O'Daly
Design Manager: David Poole
Designer: Kim Browne
Picture Manager: Sophie Mortimer
Production Director: Alastair Gourlay

Dewey no. 509

ISBN: 978 1 4451 4257 9

Printed in China

Franklin Watts
An imprint of
Hachette Children's Group
Part of the Watts Publishing Group
Carmelite House
50 Victoria Embankment
London EC4Y 0DZ

An Hachette UK company
www.hachette.co.uk

www.franklinwatts.co.uk

Contents

Introduction

The decades following World War II have seen science advance rapidly, with breakthroughs happening faster than would have seemed possible in earlier times.

A consumer revolution meant that more people wanted to buy more products, encouraging commercial development. Educational institutions funded medical research that could benefit public health, including a better understanding of genetics and how they might be manipulated.

Science and Politics

The advance of science became caught up in the Cold War, the ideological stand-off between the capitalist United States on the one hand and the communist Soviet Union on the other. One result was the space race, in which the United States travelled to the Moon as a demonstration of its technological superiority. At the end of the Cold War, the former enemies and other nations joined in research into the solar system and beyond.

The first space missions were worked out largely with pen and paper. By the end of the century, huge computers planned and monitored all aspects of each mission. By then, computers were everywhere. They were introduced originally as calculating machines, but the type of data they handled had broadened, and the speed at which they operated grew faster. The Internet linked all of the world's computers and allowed knowledge to spread rapidly around the globe.

About This Book

This book uses timelines to describe scientific and technological advances from the post-World War II boom that began around 1950 to about 2014. A continuous timeline of the period runs along the bottom of all the pages. Its entries are colour-coded to indicate the different fields of science to which they belong. Each chapter also has its own subject timeline, which runs vertically down the side of the page.

The Space Shuttle waits on its launch pad in Florida. The shuttle was the first reusable spacecraft. Among its missions from 1981 to 2011 were voyages to supply the International Space Station.

The First Computers

A computer is an electronic machine that handles its data in the form of digits, or numbers, expressed in binary notation, 1 and 0.

Binary is a number system that uses only two digits, 1 and 0, represented in the computer's activities and memory as on and off pulses of electric current. The first computers were used by the US Army and Navy near the end of World War II (1939–1945). These massive vacuum-tube machines were developed from electronic calculating machines of the late 1930s, which in turn derived from mechanical calculating machines.

The first calculator was the abacus, a frame with beads invented in about

↑ The difference engine designed by Charles Babbage (see right) was built after his death and found to work as he planned.

TIMELINE
1950–1952

KEY:

- Astronomy and Maths
- Biology and Medicine
- Chemistry and Physics
- Engineering and Invention

1950 English physicians establish a link between tobacco smoking and cancer.

1950 Dutch astronomer Jan Oort suggests the existence of the Oort cloud, which extends into space around the Solar System; it is home to all long-period comets.

1951 US researchers at the Eastman Kodak Company discover what will become known as 'superglue'.

1950

1951

1950 US physicist James Rainwater proposes a new model of the atomic nucleus, whose shape is not perfectly spherical but distorted.

1950 English mathematician Alan Turing proposes a test to determine whether a computer has real intelligence (whether it can 'think').

1951 US chemist Linus Pauling discovers the spiral structure of some proteins.

→ The slide rule was in regular use until the 1970s, when electronic calculators appeared.

Timeline

1833 Babbage designs his 'analytical engine'

1890 Hollerith produces punched cards

1942 The electronic calculator appears

1946 ENIAC and Neumann's stored-program computer

1951 First mass-produced computer (UNIVAC I)

3000 BCE and still used in parts of China and Japan. The task of multiplication is simplified by logarithms, invented in 1614 by Scottish mathematician John Napier and 'mechanised' in the slide rule designed in 1622 by English mathematician William Oughtred.

Prototype Computers

French scientist Blaise Pascal probably invented the first mechanical adding machine in 1642. It had a system of intermeshed cogs, a method also adopted by English mathematician Charles Babbage in his 'analytical engine' of 1833. Babbage's machine could be programmed for a particular calculation and was therefore a computer (although it was not electronic). From the 1880s, inventors such as the American William Burroughs developed calculating machines with keyboards – called comptometers. Later versions of such machines also provided a printout of the results.

→ Blaise Pascal, inventor of the adding machine, also experimented with the mercury barometer.

1951 US computer pioneers John Mauchly and John Eckert build UNIVAC 1, the first commercial computer in the United States.

1952 US physician Jonas Salk develops a vaccine against polio.

1952 A De Havilland Comet makes the first scheduled flight by a jet airliner (from London to Johannesburg).

1952   1953

1951 US astronomer William Morgan provides evidence that our galaxy (the Milky Way) is a typical spiral galaxy.

1952 US government scientists explode the first hydrogen bomb.

1952 US mathematician Grace Hopper writes a compiler computer program, A–O.

Jacquard's First 'Programs'

French weaver Joseph Jacquard invented the first 'programs' long before computers existed. Jacquard designed a textile loom that he programmed with a sequence of cards with lines of holes punched in them. Each line on the card corresponded to a line in the cloth. Each hole dictated whether one of the hooks on the loom head was up or down. The hooks carried thread that was therefore either present or absent from the woven cloth, creating the coloured pattern.

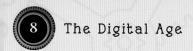

← Punched cards were used for programming on early computers.

Early methods of feeding data into programmable machines mainly used punched tape or punched cards. Around 1805, French weaver Joseph Jacquard designed a loom that could weave various patterns in carpets by following instructions on an endless belt of punched cards. American inventor Herman Hollerith used similar cards to record and analyse results of the 1890 US census. The company that Hollerith formed later became part of International Business Machines (IBM).

The Entrance of Electronics

Electromechanical calculators appeared in the 1930s, invented by US scientists such as Vannevar Bush and John Atanasoff. By 1942, Atanasoff constructed an electronic calculator (the ABC) using vacuum tubes that could be programmed to process data. This was arguably the first true computer. At Harvard in the United States in 1944, Howard Aiken produced a manually operated digital machine controlled by punched paper tape. In 1946, the all-electronic ENIAC (Electronic Numerical Integrator and Calculator) computer came into use, although it still used vacuum tubes.

TIMELINE
1953–1955

KEY:

- Astronomy and Maths
- Biology and Medicine
- Chemistry and Physics
- Engineering and Invention

1953 Soviet scientists test their first hydrogen bomb.

1953 Biophysicists Francis Crick, Maurice Wilkins and James Watson, supported by the work of physical chemist Rosalind Franklin, determine the structure of the DNA molecule.

1954 A successful field test of Jonas Salk's polio vaccine is held in the United States.

1953

1954

1953 English engineer Christopher Cockerell begins to develop the hovercraft.

1953 US surgeon John Gibbo Jr performs the first successful open-heart surgery on a human patient.

1954 US lorry operator Malcolm MacLean introduces standard-sized transport containers.

At Princeton in the United States in 1946, mathematician John von Neumann built the first machine with a stored program that used binary numbers. The idea was incorporated into UNIVAC I, the first computer to be manufactured in quantity in 1951. In 1949, a team at Manchester University, England, built a machine with a stored program under English mathematician Alan Turing. Turing's machine was so successful the British government sold eight of the Mark 1 computers – a large number at the time.

After the invention of the transistor in the late 1940s, computers became faster and smaller. By the 1960s, silicon chips arrived, enabling circuits designed in 1970 to incorporate a complete computer microprocessor on a single chip. Microchips are now used in personal computers (PCs), domestic appliances, cars and industrial robots.

This is the control panel of a UNIVAC I computer. The UNIVAC I was used to tabulate the results of the 1954 US census.

1954 US electronics engineer Gordon Teal develops the silicon transistor, which is much cheaper than the earlier germanium transistors.

1955 Indian scientist Narinder Kapany develops optical fibres for carrying light over long distances.

1955 Bell Laboratories build the first computer using transistors instead of vacuum tubes.

1955

1956

1954 French inventor Marc Grégoire invents the non-stick frying pan.

1955 US scientists at General Electric produce small synthetic diamonds from graphite.

1955 The British company Rolls-Royce develops an experimental vertical take off and landing (VTOL) aircraft.

DNA: The Double Helix

Before the 1950s, scientists already knew genes carried on chromosomes were the units of inheritance. These chromosomes are a mixture of proteins and DNA.

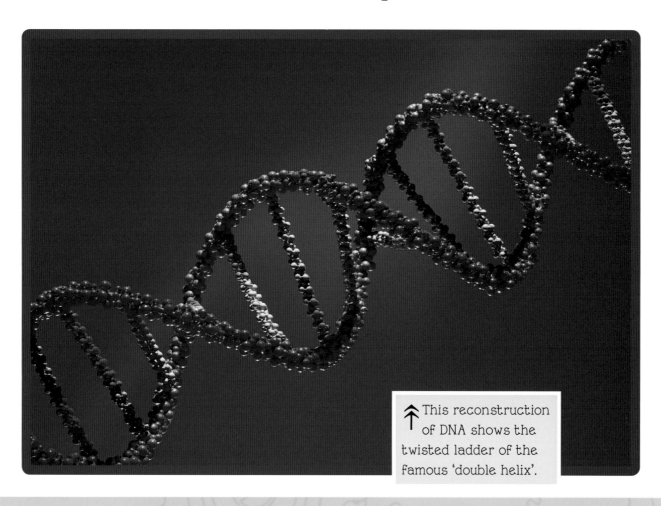

↑ This reconstruction of DNA shows the twisted ladder of the famous 'double helix'.

TIMELINE
1956–1958

1956 US physicists Clyde Cowan and Frederick Reines discover the neutrino, a subatomic particle.

1956 US computer programmers at IBM devise the FORTRAN computer language.

1957 US physicist Eugene Parker discovers the solar wind, streams of particles ejected from the Sun.

KEY:

- Astronomy and Maths
- Biology and Medicine
- Chemistry and Physics
- Engineering and Invention

1956

1957

1956 US physician Edward Thomas carries out the first successful bone marrow transplant operation.

1956 The company Ampex markets a videotape recorder, designed by US electronics engineer Alexander Poniatoff.

1957 Commercial production of polypropene plastic begins in Italy.

In 1951, American Linus Pauling described a class of proteins whose molecules took the form of a helix (a three-dimensional spiral). He then looked at DNA (deoxyribonucleic acid).

Watson and Crick

For Francis Crick at Cambridge, England, the structure of DNA was an obsession. He and James Watson began working on it. Their work remained low key. Competition between the great research institutions was frowned on, and deciphering the structure of DNA was also the aim of scientists at King's College, London. There, Maurice Wilkins and Rosalind Franklin were doing a series of experiments using X-ray diffraction to find DNA's structure. Franklin did not think DNA might be a helix, but Watson and Crick did. In 1951, they produced a model of DNA as a triple helix. Franklin disagreed, as the structure did not conform to her data. Watson and Crick started again. In 1952, Linus Pauling presented his model,

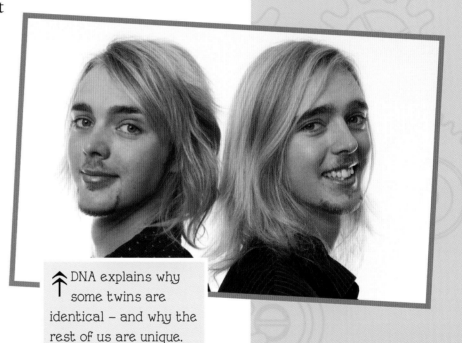

↑ DNA explains why some twins are identical – and why the rest of us are unique.

Timeline

1951 Pauling describes helical proteins

1953 Watson and Crick write papers describing the double helix structure of DNA

1973 The first genetically engineered organism is created

1982 Genetically engineered insulin is produced

1957 Soviet scientists launch the first artificial satellites to orbit Earth, *Sputnik I* and *Sputnik II*.

1958 US microbiologist John Enders produces a vaccine against measles.

1958 Scottish surgeon Ian Donald introduces the use of an ultrasound scan to examine an unborn baby in its mother's womb.

1958   1959

1957 The rotary Wankel engine, invented by Felix Wankel, goes into production in West Germany.

1958 In the United States, the National Aeronautics and Space Administration (NASA) is founded.

1958 US electronic engineers invent integrated circuits, which enable a great reduction in the size of circuits for computers and electronic devices.

The Secret of Replication

When the strands of the double helix separate, the bases that link the strands are exposed. Spare nucleotides are drawn to the two unzipped strands and link up to form new strands. The bases always pair up in the same way (A to T and G to C), so they produce two double helices identical to the original. Rarely, something goes wrong with the copying process and a mutation takes place, meaning that one of the new strands differs from the original.

When not undergoing replication, DNA is tightly coiled and packed into structures called chromosomes.

Replication in action: DNA strands are 'unzipped' by enzymes, and each strand acts as a template for a new double helix.

⟹ The rungs of the DNA 'ladder' are made up of pairs of bases.

Bases on free nucleotides pair with exposed bases on an unzipped chain and link to form a new strand. Base pairings are always consistent.

T
G
A
A
C
C
T
G

but he had also got it wrong.

DNA contains four different chemical compounds (bases): adenine (A), cytosine (C), guanine (G) and thymine (T). The realisation that they paired off in a predictable way set Watson and Crick on the right track.

Using Genetic Engineering

By the early 1950s, a number of discoveries took place concerning bacterial plasmids, which are tiny circlets

TIMELINE
1959–1961

1959 Soviet scientists send three Lunik probes to the Moon.

1959 The German company Voigtlander produces a zoom lens for its cameras.

1960 Kenyan anthropologist Jonathan Leakey discovers remains of the oldest-known human, *Homo habilis* ('handy man'), in Tanzania.

KEY:

Astronomy and Maths

Biology and Medicine

Chemistry and Physics

Engineering and Invention

1959

1960

1959 Greek-British engineer Alec Issigonis designs the Mini car.

1959 French physician Jérôme Lejeune establishes that the condition Down's syndrome is caused by a chromosome defect.

1960 US chemist Robert Woodward synthesises the green plant pigment, chlorophyll.

of DNA that are easily isolated and manipulated and can be reinserted into cells in a modified form. They provided one of modern genetics' most important tools.

In 1968, Stuart Linn and Werner Arber discovered restriction enzymes that 'cut' DNA in certain places. The cut ends bind back together or splice with the ends of other sections of DNA. In 1969, Jonathan Beckwith isolated a single gene. This made it possible to delete or insert new genes into a sequence of DNA. In 1973, Stanley Cohen and Herbert Boyer removed a section of DNA and replaced it with a gene from a different bacterium. This was the first genetically engineered organism.

Genetic engineering allows scientists to replace undesirable genes with desirable ones. Debate continues over these techniques, and there is some mistrust of genetically modified (GM) organisms. Hopes that gene replacement therapies would provide treatment for genetic disorders are closer to being realised after decades of research.

↑ Genetic engineering has allowed the development of new strands of food crops.

1960 US physicist Theodore H. Maiman invents the ruby laser, the first practical laser.

1961 Soviet cosmonaut Yuri Gagarin becomes the first person in space.

1961 US chemists isolate the new radioactive element lawrencium.

1961

1962

1960 US zoologists discover that bottle-nosed dolphins use a form of echolocation to detect objects underwater.

1961 The US company Texas Instruments produces the first silicon chips (for computers).

1961 The IBM corporation markets the 'golfball' typewriter.

Lasers

A laser beam cuts metal more precisely than a saw. Lasers are used in delicate eye surgery and to measure distances. Without lasers there would be no DVDs or Blu-ray.

↑ Among the most familiar uses of lasers are spectacular light shows.

TIMELINE
1962–1964

KEY:

- Astronomy and Maths
- Biology and Medicine
- Chemistry and Physics
- Engineering and Invention

1962

1963

1962 Astronaut John Glenn becomes the first American in space.

1962 The 7-bit, 128-character American Standard Code for Information Interchange (ASCII) is introduced; it later becomes the international standard.

1963 Dutch company Philips introduces audiocassette tapes.

1962 The first ring-pull can goes on sale in the United States.

1962 In her book *Silent Spring*, US writer Rachel Carson highlights the damaging environmental effects of chemical pesticides.

1963 US researchers develop the chemistry for producing 'instant' colour photographs.

In 1917, German-American physicist Albert Einstein recognised that it should be possible to stimulate atoms and molecules so they send out light. That is the principle behind the laser. It was not until the 1950s that physicists suggested a device that could generate a laser beam. In 1952, US physicist Charles H. Townes described a way to stimulate molecules of ammonia to give off microwave radiation using the principle of the maser: microwave amplification by stimulated emission of radiation. He built the first maser in 1953.

The First Lasers

Microwave radiation is invisible, but in 1958 Townes and Arthur Schawlow showed it was theoretically possible to make a device to emit visible light. It would produce light amplification by stimulated emission of radiation – the laser. The American Theodore H. Maiman made the first laser in 1960.

When a substance absorbs energy, its atoms or molecules jump from a low-energy level to a high-energy level. As they drop back to the low-energy level, they release surplus energy in the form of light. Ordinarily, each atom or molecule emits light independently and at different wavelengths. But if the

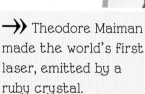 Theodore Maiman made the world's first laser, emitted by a ruby crystal.

Timeline

1917 Einstein proposes stimulated emission

1952 Townes conceives maser

1958 Laser proposed in theory

1960 Maiman builds the ruby laser

1963 British chemist Leslie Phillips develops a method of manufacturing carbon fibres.

1964 In Japan, the first bullet trains achieve speeds of 160 km/h (100 mph).

1964 The longest suspension bridge in the world at the time opens over the Verrazano Narrows between Brooklyn and Staten Island, New York.

1964

1965

1964 NASA's probe *Mariner 4* sends back photographs of the surface of Mars.

1964 US engineer Robert Moog invents a music synthesiser.

1964 US radio astronomers Arno Penzias and Robert Wilson detect cosmic background microwave radiation; it convinces most astronomers that the Big Bang theory is correct.

substance is exposed to very intense light of a particular wavelength during its brief instant at the high-energy level, it will emit light at the same wavelength as the light shining on it. That is how the substance is stimulated, and stimulation further intensifies the light. The next step is to amplify the light by the use of mirrors. A mirror at one end of the device reflects light back through the substance being stimulated. A half-silvered mirror at the opposite end reflects some of the light but allows the remainder to escape as a laser beam.

A Focused Beam

A laser emits a narrow beam of light of a single wavelength – and therefore one colour – in which all the waves are in step. The light beam from a torch or car headlight diverges, so it illuminates a large area. A laser beam, however, is more focused. When it strikes a surface, the surface absorbs some of its energy and its temperature rises. Lasers produce such strong heat over such a small area that they can be used to trim excess material from electronic components and even to perform surgery on the retina at the back of the eye.

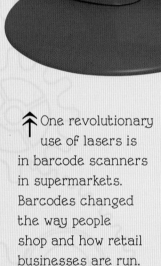

↑ One revolutionary use of lasers is in barcode scanners in supermarkets. Barcodes changed the way people shop and how retail businesses are run.

TIMELINE
1965–1967

KEY:

- Astronomy and Maths
- Biology and Medicine
- Chemistry and Physics
- Engineering and Invention

1965

1966

1965 Soviet cosmonaut Alexei Leonov is the first person to walk in space.

1965 The Mont Blanc road tunnel opens between France and Italy.

1966 Soviet and US space probes land on the Moon.

1965 American Digital Equipment Corporation introduces the first minicomputer.

1965 American physicists Moo-Young Han and Yoichiro Nambu introduce 'colour' as a way of classifying some aspects of subatomic particles.

1966 Chinese and British engineers invent fibre-optic cable.

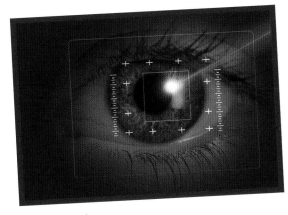

Narrow laser beams can also measure distances. When a pulse strikes a surface, some of it is reflected. The speed of light is always the same, so distance is calculated from the time that elapses between the emission of the pulse and the arrival of its reflection. This is called lidar (light radar). Lidar is also used to measure the speed of moving objects, including road traffic in law enforcement.

↑ Laser surgery on the eye can correct optical defects in a matter of seconds.

Producing the Ruby Laser

Both ends of a cylindrical rod of ruby crystal are polished flat and coated with silver to make a mirror at one end and a partial mirror at the other. The ruby is enclosed in a jacket to keep it cool. A spiral tube surrounding the ruby emits flashes of light. (Alternatively, the light can lie beside the ruby or be reflected onto it by mirrors.) Atoms in the ruby absorb energy from the tube and emit light. The laser beam emerges from the partially silvered end of the tube.

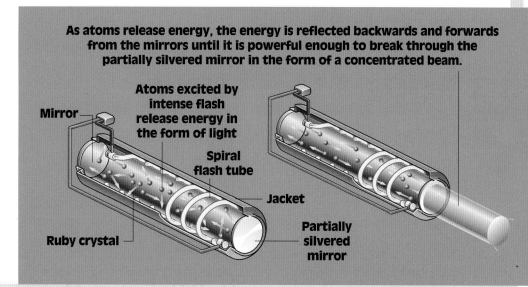

As atoms release energy, the energy is reflected backwards and forwards from the mirrors until it is powerful enough to break through the partially silvered mirror in the form of a concentrated beam.

Atoms excited by intense flash release energy in the form of light

Mirror

Spiral flash tube

Jacket

Ruby crystal

Partially silvered mirror

1966 US inventor Stephanie Kwolek invents the ultrastrong synthetic fibre Kevlar. Five times stronger than steel, its uses include bulletproof vests.

1967 Three US astronauts die in a fire during a ground test of an Apollo spacecraft.

1967 South African surgeon Christiaan Barnard performs the first human heart transplant operation. The patient lives for 18 days with the new heart.

1967

1968

1966 An electronic fuel-injection system for car engines is invented in Britain.

1967 British astronomers Jocelyn Bell Burnell and Antony Hewish detect the first pulsar.

1967 The US company Raytheon markets the first domestic microwave oven.

Semiconductors

Modern cars are fitted with 'chips' that perform lots of different tasks. Chips are all around us, but without semiconductors, they could not exist.

→ An integrated circuit has semiconductor devices – transistors, diodes, capacitors and resistors – made as a single unit on a silicon chip.

TIMELINE
1968–1970

KEY:

Astronomy and Maths

Biology and Medicine

Chemistry and Physics

Engineering and Invention

1968

1969

1968 NASA's *Apollo 7* orbits Earth; *Apollo 8* orbits the Moon.

1968 Italian-American inventor Candido Jacuzzi invents the whirlpool bath named after him.

1969 *Apollo 11* makes the first manned Moon landing.

1968 US computer engineer Douglas Engelbart devises the computer mouse.

1968 The Lockheed C-5 Galaxy becomes the largest aeroplane in the world.

1969 The Anglo-French supersonic airliner *Concorde* makes its maiden flight in France.

Most metals conduct electricity well. Electrical wires are often made of copper, for example. Substances such as glass, paper and rubber conduct electricity very badly and are used to insulate electrical wiring. Between these two groups is a class of substances called semiconductors. Germanium, tin, selenium, zinc and tellurium are semiconducting elements, but silicon is by far the most widely used semiconductor material.

The First Semiconductor

When Italian inventor Guglielmo Marconi was experimenting with converting an electrical current into radio waves, he needed a device to detect incoming radio signals. This rectifier, which allows a current to flow in one direction but not the other, was built by German inventor Ferdinand Braun in 1874. It was the first semiconductor device.

Rectifiers have two terminals, but advances in radio technology required devices with three terminals, allowing the current or voltage between two of the terminals to be controlled by the current or voltage applied to the third. The first three-terminal devices were vacuum-tube triodes, called valves. Later versions had several triodes enclosed in the same tube. Valves used large amounts of power and became very hot. Their metal parts burned out, causing the valve to fail.

Timeline

1874 Braun's rectifier

1947 Point-contact transistor

1948 Audio amplifier

1948 Junction transistor

1958 Integrated circuit

1959 Planar technology

⬆ Old-style valves had to warm up before they would begin to work.

1969 English chemist Dorothy Hodgkin uses X-ray crystallography to work out the molecular structure of insulin.

1970 Floppy disk data storage media come into use for computers.

1970 Fossil finds in Antarctica, Africa and India provide evidence for the theory of continental drift, showing that these landmasses must once have been joined.

1970

1971

1969 English scientists Robert Edwards and Patrick Steptoe fertilise the first human eggs in vitro.

1970 The 400-seat Boeing 747 jumbo jet goes into service.

1970 NASA's *Apollo 13* mission is abandoned after an accident in space, but the crew return safely to Earth.

Semiconductors

In a junction diode, current can flow only one way across the junction. There is a steady flow of holes and electrons to the junction; they neutralise each other. The positive and negative charges cancel and there is no charge overall. As a result, current flows freely. If the connections are reversed, the battery draws the electrons and holes away from the junction, and they can go no further.

➤➤ N-type semiconductors have free electrons; p-type semiconductors have vacancies (holes).

In 1947, US physicists William Shockley, John Bardeen and Walter Brattain made the first solid three-terminal device – a transistor – using germanium. In 1948 they wired several transistors to other components to make an audio amplifier. Unlike valve amplifiers, theirs did not need to warm up to work. Shockley also conceived the junction transistor, made from slices of a semiconductor pressed together, in 1948.

The presence of impurities in the germanium crystal improved its semiconductor properties. Modern semiconductors are made from slices of silicon crystal with impurities added in tiny quantities.

The next development came in 1958. Jack Kilby, an American electronic engineer working at Texas Instruments, realised that, rather than making transistors one at a time, impurities could be overlaid to make several transistors on the same semiconductor. Other components

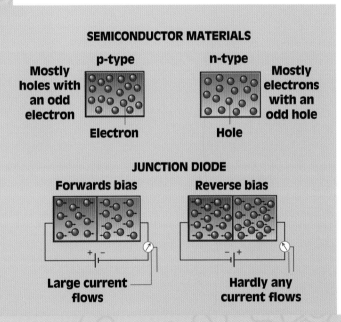

SEMICONDUCTOR MATERIALS

p-type — Mostly holes with an odd electron — Electron

n-type — Mostly electrons with an odd hole — Hole

JUNCTION DIODE

Forwards bias — Large current flows

Reverse bias — Hardly any current flows

could be added. This was the first integrated circuit.

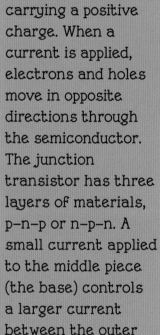

→» Integrated circuits contain all the pieces of a traditional circuit board.

Silicon Chips

A year later, at Fairchild Semiconductor Corporation, Jean Hoerni and Robert Noyce developed planar technology. This process spreads different layers onto a wafer of silicon to make a flat transistor, then places metal strips onto the surface to make the necessary connections.

Smaller than postage stamps, the chips in computers, MP4 players and other electronic devices are plastic cases enclosing layers of transistors and related components, together with the wiring linking them, on the surface of a sliver of silicon. They are integrated circuits based on semiconductor technology.

Adding Impurities

'Doping' an element with impurities produces n- or p-type semiconductors. The first have free electrons; the second have vacancies (holes) carrying a positive charge. When a current is applied, electrons and holes move in opposite directions through the semiconductor. The junction transistor has three layers of materials, p–n–p or n–p–n. A small current applied to the middle piece (the base) controls a larger current between the outer pieces (the emitter and the collector).

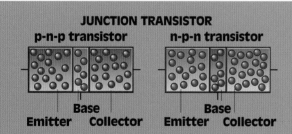

JUNCTION TRANSISTOR
p-n-p transistor   n-p-n transistor
Base   Base
Emitter Collector Emitter Collector

«← A junction transistor can be used in amplifiers and other circuits.

1972 US theoretical physicist Murray Gell-Mann develops a new branch of physics, quantum chromodynamics (QCD). It describes nuclear interaction in terms of quarks.

1973 US physicists at Bell Laboratories produce a continuous-wave laser that can be tuned to different wavelengths.

1973 The first teletext systems are broadcast on British television.

1973   1974

1972 The computer company Atari, Inc., creates the popular video game 'Pong'. It is followed a year later by the first computer video game.

1973 US and English physicists begin to develop nuclear magnetic resonance imaging (MRI scanning), later used in medical analysis.

1973 NASA space probe *Pioneer 10* flies by Jupiter.

The Apollo Programme

In 1961, President John F. Kennedy pledged the United
States would land a man on the Moon within ten years.
In July 1969, two astronauts fulfilled that promise.

→» The astronauts
from *Apollo 11* erect
a flag on the Moon.
The flag is supported
by wire as there is no
wind to blow it open.

TIMELINE
1974–1976

KEY:

- Astronomy and Maths
- Biology and Medicine
- Chemistry and Physics
- Engineering and Invention

1974 US company General Motors introduces catalytic converters for cars.

1974 US chemical engineer Arthur Fry invents the semi-adhesive Post-it Note.

1975 British pharmacologists discover enkephalins, chemicals produced in the brain that control pain.

1974

1975

1974 NASA space probe *Mariner 10* reaches Mercury.

1974 US scientists issue warnings about the damage CFCs (chlorofluorocarbons) are doing to Earth's ozone layer.

1975 Soviet and US space capsules link up in Earth orbit.

The spacecraft that launched the *Apollo 11* astronauts to the Moon had four main parts. The Saturn V rocket propelled the whole thing into space; the command module, *Columbia*, housed the three astronauts; the service module contained the main propulsion rockets for the journey; and below that was the lunar module, *Eagle*. The lunar module carried two of the three astronauts down to land on the Moon's surface on the Sea of Tranquillity. After they had completed their surface mission, they took off again in *Eagle*, which returned to dock with the orbiting command module. Just eight days later, it parachuted into the Pacific Ocean.

The Apollo Programme

The earlier Apollo missions had tested various launch procedures, rockets and modules – at first in Earth orbit, then around the Moon – before making the final landing. In January 1967, the first planned Apollo flight ended in disaster when three astronauts died in a fire

Timeline

1967 January: Three Apollo astronauts die in ground fire

1968 October: *Apollo 7* in Earth orbit

1968 December: *Apollo 8* orbits the Moon

1969 March: *Apollo 9* tests lunar module in Earth orbit

1969 May: *Apollo 10* tests lunar module in Moon orbit

1969 July: *Apollo 11* lands on the Moon

← *Apollo 11* lifts off in 1969. The top of the giant Saturn V rocket carried the command, service and lunar modules and an escape tower, which could blast away the command module and crew in case of an emergency.

1975 US engineer Edward Roberts markets the first commercial personal computer (PC), the Altair 8800.

1976 The supersonic airliner *Concorde* goes into commercial service.

1976 US physiologist Roger Guillemin reports the existence of endorphins, morphine-like chemicals released in the brain to control pain.

1976

1977

1975 US computer programmers Bill Gates and Paul Allen found the Microsoft Corporation.

1976 In Japan, the Matsushita company introduces the VHS format for video cassettes.

1976 US computer designers Steven Jobs and Stephen Wozniak found the computer company Apple.

Stepping Stones to the Moon

Apollo 11 took off on 16 July, 1969. The three stages of the Saturn V rocket fired (steps 1, 2, 3) to send the spacecraft into Earth orbit and launch the modules on the path to the Moon (4). Once in Moon orbit, the lunar module separated from the command module (5) and descended to the surface (6). After the landing, the top part of the lunar module took off (7) and rejoined the command module (8), to follow the transearth trajectory. After jettisoning the lunar module (9), the command module re-entered Earth's atmosphere (10) and parachuted into the Pacific Ocean (11).

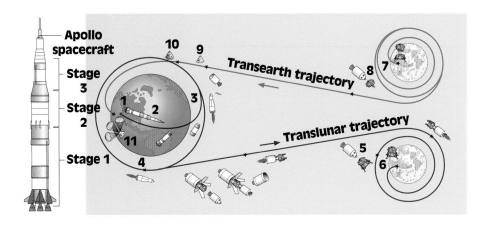

↑ This diagram shows the stages of the Saturn V rocket and the Moon mission.

during a launch pad test. The next year, NASA (National Aeronautics and Space Administration) made three uncrewed launches. In October 1968, *Apollo 7* carried three astronauts on a 163-orbit flight around Earth. Two months later, *Apollo 8* took three astronauts to the Moon, making ten orbits. In March 1969, the lunar module was tested in Earth orbit by *Apollo 9.* In May, two *Apollo 10* astronauts tested it in a low orbit around the Moon.

The Moon Landing

Apollo 11 lifted off on 16 July 1969 crewed by Neil Armstrong, Edwin (Buzz) Aldrin and Michael Collins. It reached the Moon without a hitch. Armstrong and Aldrin descended to the surface in the lunar module on 20 July, spending two hours taking photographs and

TIMELINE
1977-1979

KEY:

- Astronomy and Maths
- Biology and Medicine
- Chemistry and Physics
- Engineering and Invention

1977 US astronomers observe the rings of Uranus.

1977 US government scientists develop a neutron bomb.

1978 Astronomers in the US locate Pluto's moon Charon.

1977

1978

1977 A pedal-powered aeroplane, *Gossamer Condor*, flies over 1.6 kilometres (1 mile).

1977 A team led by British biochemists explains the first full sequence of DNA bases (of a virus).

1978 The US government bans the use of CFCs (chlorofluorocarbons) in aerosol cans.

collecting samples. They erected an American flag and left a plaque marking their mission.

Later Missions

Apollo 12 landed on the Moon later in 1969, but *Apollo 13* in April 1970 was a near-disaster. An explosion in the service module cut off power and oxygen, but the crew still made a safe re-entry. *Apollo 17* in December 1972 was NASA's last crewed trip to the Moon.

The Apollo programme cost about £16 billion. That makes the 382 kilograms (842 lbs) of Moon rock brought back to Earth worth over £41.9 million per kilogram!

⟩⟩ Earth rises above the surface of the Moon in a photo taken from *Apollo 11.*

The Apollo Modules

During take-off and re-entry, the crew stayed in the command module. The attached service module contained the engine and fuel to get to the Moon and back. The lunar module had two sections: the lower part stayed on the Moon while the upper part carried the astronauts back to the orbiting command module. The lunar module and service modules were jettisoned, allowing the command module to re-enter Earth's atmosphere and splash down.

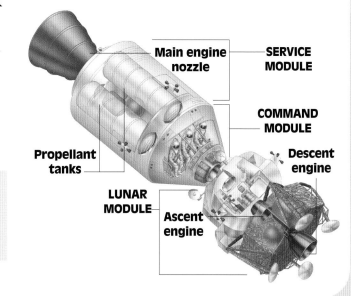

Main engine nozzle — **SERVICE MODULE**

COMMAND MODULE

Propellant tanks

Descent engine

LUNAR MODULE

Ascent engine

⟩⟩ The service, command and lunar modules configured for Moon orbit.

1978 The first 'test tube' baby is born in England.

1979 Digital compact discs (CDs) are developed independently in Japan and the Netherlands.

1979 The earliest cases of the disease that becomes known as AIDS (acquired immunity deficiency syndrome) occur in the United States.

1979

1978 US surgeon Robert Jarvik devises the Jarvik-7 artificial heart.

1979 The Swedish company Ericsson markets the first cellular telephones (mobile phones).

1979 The World Health Organization announces that smallpox has been eradicated worldwide.

The Space Shuttle

The story of the Space Shuttle is one of triumph and tragedy. It was involved in some of NASA's greatest space achievements as well as in its two worst disasters.

← Space Shuttle *Discovery* takes off from the Kennedy Space Center, Florida, in September 1988. It was the first flight since the *Challenger* had blown up two years earlier.

TIMELINE
1980–1982

KEY:

- Astronomy and Maths
- Biology and Medicine
- Chemistry and Physics
- Engineering and Invention

1980

1981

1980 The US Supreme Court rules that genetically engineered life forms can be patented.

1980 US father and son Luis and Walter Alvarez suggest that a meteorite collision with Earth may have led to the extinction of the dinosaurs.

1981 US authorities first acknowledge acquired immune deficiency syndrome (AIDS) as a communicable disease.

1980 Sony in Japan and Philips in the Netherlands market the audio compact disc (CD) for commercial use.

1980 Polish-American mathematician Benoit Mandlebrot investigates fractals, which are mathematical curves generated by successive subdivision.

1981 US company Hewlett Packard launches a 32-bit silicon chip for its computers.

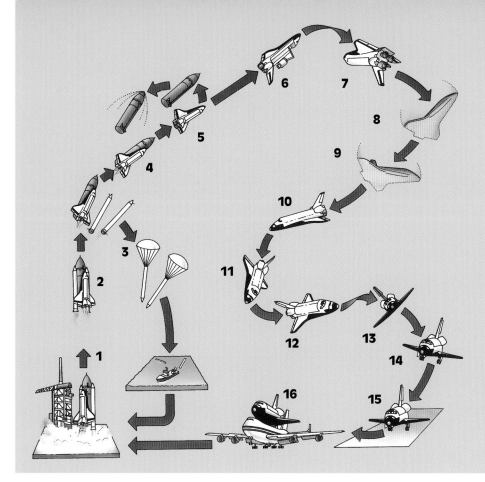

← After lift-off (1), the shuttle accelerates upwards (2) for two minutes before dropping the empty booster rockets (3), which parachute down to be recovered. About eight minutes into the flight (4), the shuttle enters Earth orbit and jettisons the external fuel tank (5), which burns up on re-entry. After its space mission (6), the shuttle turns around (7), fires its rockets for braking (8), and re-enters Earth's atmosphere (9). After turning again (10), it swings from side to side (11, 12) to lose speed before making the landing approach (13) and gliding down (14) to land on its wheels (15), stopping with the aid of a braking parachute. The carrier aircraft (16) takes the shuttle back to Edwards Air Force Base for preparation for the next flight.

Plans for the Space Shuttle date back to 1972. NASA wanted a cargo-carrying spacecraft that could go into space, carry out its mission and then return to base to land on its own and be used again and again. It was hoped the shuttle would fly up to 50 missions a year, but in reality it flew only about eight.

At launch, the shuttle consisted of three parts. The aeroplane-like orbiter was 37 metres (122 feet) long and had three main engines fuelled by liquid oxygen and

1981 NASA's first space shuttle, *Columbia*, makes its maiden flight, proving that a reusable spacecraft is practicable.

1982 Two Soviet space probes reach Venus and sample the atmosphere.

1982 Engineers in the United States build the world's largest solar power plant, Solar One.

1982

1981 French railway company SNCF introduces its new high-speed train, the TGV (Train à Grande Vitesse).

1982 Biochemists produce the first totally synthetic vaccine (against diphtheria).

1982 Biologist Karl Setter discovers bacteria living in hot seawater near black smokers on the seabed.

liquid hydrogen. The large external tank held extra fuel, and two 45-metre (148-foot) solid rocket boosters attached to either side of it. The flight deck held up to seven crew, and the mid-deck served as a canteen, kitchen and gym, and also had a toilet. The 18-metre (59-foot) payload bay carried up to 25 tonnes (27.6 tons). The bay also had a robot arm that deployed and retrieved payloads and acted as a 'ladder' for spacewalking astronauts.

Shuttle Missions

NASA built six Space Shuttles. The first, *Enterprise* of 1977, was never launched into space. In 1981, *Columbia* became the first shuttle to make an orbital flight, followed by *Challenger* in 1983, *Discovery* in 1984 and *Atlantis* in 1985. In 1986, *Challenger* exploded soon after launch, killing all seven crew members. NASA then built *Endeavour*, which

Milestone Shuttle Missions

Year	Shuttle	Mission
1983	*Challenger*	Sally Ride becomes first American woman in space
1984	*Challenger*	Bruce McCandless makes first untethered space walk
1989	*Atlantis*	Sends *Magellan* space probe towards Venus
1989	*Atlantis*	Sends *Galileo* space probe towards Jupiter
1990	*Discovery*	Places the Hubble Space Telescope in Earth orbit
1990	*Discovery*	Sends *Ulysses* space probe towards the Sun
1993	*Endeavour*	Corrects a fault in the Hubble Space Telescope's mirror
1995	*Atlantis*	100th US crewed flight
1996	*Atlantis*	Docks with Russian space station *Mir*
1996	*Columbia*	At almost 17 days, longest Space Shuttle mission
1997	*Discovery*	Five space walks in servicing the Hubble Space Telescope
1998	*Discovery*	John Glenn (age 77) returns to space after 36 years
1999	*Discovery*	Fixes fault with gyroscopes on the Hubble Space Telescope
2002	*Columbia*	Upgrades the Hubble Space Telescope
2005	*Discovery*	Docks with the new International Space Station
2009	*Atlantis*	Last Hubble Space Telescope servicing mission
2010	*Discovery*	Last Space Shuttle night launch
2011	*Atlantis*	Final flight of the Space Shuttle

TIMELINE
1983–1985

KEY:

- Astronomy and Maths
- Biology and Medicine
- Chemistry and Physics
- Engineering and Invention

1983

1984

1983 US astronaut Sally Ride becomes the first American woman in space.

1983 US mathematicians announce a new way of finding prime numbers.

1984 US biologist Robert Sinsheimer proposes the setting up of the Human Genome Project.

1983 US company Apple markets a home computer that uses a mouse and pull-down menus.

1983 French virologist Luc Montagnier and US physician Robert Gallo discover the human immunodeficiency virus (HIV) that causes AIDS.

1984 English geneticist Alec Jeffreys perfects the technique of genetic fingerprinting.

← The Hubble Space Telescope undergoes repairs in the shuttle's cargo bay.

first flew in 1992. In 2003, the shuttle had its second disaster when *Columbia* disintegrated 16 minutes before it was due to land. All the crew died. After a major refit, *Discovery* restarted the shuttle programme in July 2005. It docked with the International Space Station, and the crew inspected damage to the craft's tiles caused by insulating foam that broke off the external tank during lift-off. NASA grounded the fleet while investigating the tile problem.

The shuttle programme resumed in August 2009, with a *Discovery* flight. The last shuttle mission was to the International Space Station in July 2011.

→ Workers recover part of the *Challenger* after the shuttle disaster of 1986.

The *Challenger* Disaster

The explosion of *Challenger* some 73 seconds after lift-off in 1986 was an enduring moment in space exploration. Many Americans were watching the launch live. They included many students following Christa McAuliffe, a teacher recruited by NASA to interest children in the mission. The cause of the disaster was traced to a failed seal in one of the solid rocket boosters, probably itself caused by the extremely cold temperatures at the launch site.

1984 Apple sells the first Macintosh computers.

1985 British scientists detect a hole in the ozone layer above Antarctica. It is blamed on chlorofluorocarbons (CFCs) in the atmosphere.

1985 Japanese company Minolta launches the world's first autofocus single-lens reflex (SLR) camera.

1985

1984 Microsoft launches the Windows operating system for personal computers (PCs).

1985 Several chemists collaborate to produce a new allotrope of carbon, buckminsterfullerene or 'buckyballs'.

1985 Sony and Philips invent the CD-ROM (compact disc read-only memory) to store digital media.

Personal Computers

In just 20 years, the personal computer progressed from being a novelty item for enthusiasts to an essential tool used every day in households all over the world.

→》 Today, laptop and desktop computers are familiar in most homes in the developed world.

TIMELINE
1986–1988

KEY:

- Astronomy and Maths
- Biology and Medicine
- Chemistry and Physics
- Engineering and Invention

1986 Space shuttle *Challenger* blows up soon after take-off, killing all seven crew members.

1986 In the United States, the first field trials are carried out with genetically engineered crops (tobacco).

1987 Japanese airlines introduce air-to-ground satellite telephones.

1986

1987

1986 Japanese manufacturers demonstrate a digital audio tape (DAT) system.

1986 European space probe *Giotto* passes within 600 km (375 miles) of Halley's comet.

1987 Soviet cosmonaut Yuri Romanenko spends a record 326 days on the space station *Mir*.

Apersonal computer (PC) is one of the most versatile and useful devices in homes all over the world. Yet PCs are relatively new. The first fully electronic computer was built in 1946 at the University of Pennsylvania in the United States. All early computers used vacuum tubes, or valves. Those machines were so huge that they filled a large room, and they were unreliable (because of tube failures). The invention of the transistor in 1947 offered a smaller, more dependable replacement for the vacuum tube, and the invention of the integrated circuit in 1958 opened up the possibility of miniaturisation.

A Computer for the Home

In 1975 the first computer appeared that was both affordable and small enough to use at home. Micro Instrumentation and Telemetry Systems (MITS) in the United States sold the Altair 8800 for $495 (£319) assembled and in kit form for just $395 (£255). The computer came without a monitor, keyboard or printer – and it had only 256 bytes of memory.

Timeline

1946 ENIAC is the first fully electronic computer

1958 The integrated circuit is introduced

1964 BASIC programming language becomes standard

1972 CP/M operating system brought in for small computers

1975 The Altair 8800 goes on sale

1980 Bill Gates develops MS-DOS

1980 Sinclair markets the ZX80

1981 IBM sells its first PC

⟵ Programmer Bill Gates of Microsoft, photographed in 1980, developed the MS-DOS operating system that was installed in most PCs from the 1980s to the mid-1990s.

1987 German chemists make an electrically conducting plastic by 'doping' polythene with iodine.

1988 The Human Genome Organisation (HUGO) is set up to promote international collaboration in the field of human genetics.

1988 US climatologist James Hansen predicts that 'greenhouse gases' in the atmosphere will lead to global warming.

1988

1987 British surgeons carry out the first heart/lung/liver triple transplant operation.

1988 The US Patent Office grants a patent for a genetically engineered mouse.

1988 ISDN (integrated services digital network) is launched in Japan as a world standard for digital communications.

The Hard Disk Drive

Accessible back-up memory is stored on hard disks inside a computer's disk drive. Data is stored as magnetic fields in areas as small as 1 micrometre (40-millionths of an inch) across. Read/write heads mounted on the ends of arms swing in and out across each disk, 'flying' a few fractions of micrometres above the surface on a cushion of air. A carriage moves the head in and out.

→ Hard disks can rotate at speeds of 160 kilometres an hour (100 mph) or more.

Computer Software

Computer software – the programs that run useful applications such as word processing or games – will work only if the computer is able to communicate with a storage device such as a disk drive. This process requires special software in the form of an operating system. In 1972, American computer scientist Gary Kildall (1942–1994) devised PL/M (Programming Language/Microprocessor). The following year, Kildall wrote software that allowed the user to read data files stored on a disk and write files onto the disk. It was the first operating system for small computers. MS-DOS was a rival system developed by Bill Gates of Microsoft in 1980.

Computers remained expensive, however, until 1980, when Clive Sinclair designed the ZX80. It cost less than £100 ready-made and could be connected to a TV receiver.

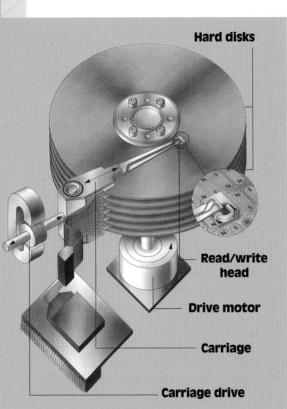

Hard disks

Read/write head

Drive motor

Carriage

Carriage drive

TIMELINE
1989–1991

KEY:

- Astronomy and Maths
- Biology and Medicine
- Chemistry and Physics
- Engineering and Invention

1989

1990

1989 The *Voyager* 2 space probe reveals that Neptune has a system of rings.

1990 NASA places the Hubble Space Telescope in orbit around Earth. It will provide astronomers with detailed images of astronomical objects.

1990 British and French engineers meet beneath the English Channel as they complete drilling for the Channel Tunnel.

1989 The oil tanker *Exxon Valdez* runs aground off Alaska, spilling millions of litres of crude oil.

1989 US computer engineer Seymour Cray sets up a company to build the Cray 3 supercomputer.

1990 English computer scientist Tim Berners-Lee begins to devise the World Wide Web.

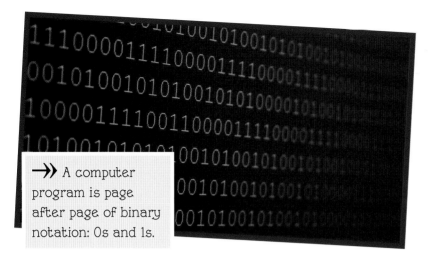

→ A computer program is page after page of binary notation: 0s and 1s.

↓ This early computer hard drive comprised a stack of hard disks mounted on the same spindle, which could all be accessed simultaneously.

IBM introduced its first small computer in 1981, calling it a 'personal computer' (PC). Within a year or two, rival manufacturers were marketing cheaper imitations, known as 'clones'. All of them resembled the IBM PC and used MS-DOS. Modern PCs are the direct descendants of the 'clones'.

Better Processors

The power of a PC depends on the speed of its processor and the amount of memory it has. Both have increased rapidly and are still doing so, allowing modern computers to perform tasks far beyond the capacity of their predecessors. The first multimedia PC appeared in 1991, and English computer scientist Tim Berners-Lee created the World Wide Web in 1990. Today, broadband web access allows users to download music and films.

1990 US company Kodak announces the invention of a Photo CD disc.

1991 Japanese researcher Sumio Iijima makes carbon nanotubes.

1991 US electronics engineer Kenneth Matsumura invents a small electrocardiograph machine that warns the wearer of heart problems.

1991

1990 The Human Genome Project begins, directed by US biophysicist James Watson.

1991 European researchers briefly achieve controlled nuclear fusion.

1991 English inventor Trevor Baylis invents a wind-up radio for use in places with no electricity supply and few batteries.

Cloning Animals

In 1996, a lamb named Dolly was born by genetic engineering. But she was not the first cloned animal. The science of cloning has a surprisingly long history.

↑ Ian Wilmut pictured with his creation, Dolly, the world's first cloned sheep.

TIMELINE
1992–1994

KEY:
- Astronomy and Maths
- Biology and Medicine
- Chemistry and Physics
- Engineering and Invention

1992

1993

1992 Experimental digital radio broadcasts begin in France.

1992 NASA scientists detect 'ripples' in cosmic background radiation (caused by minute temperature variations).

1993 US physicians introduce gene therapy for the congenital disorder cystic fibrosis.

1992 Dutch company Philips makes the interactive CD-I computer disk.

1992 US research scientists make extra-hard diamonds using the isotope carbon-13 (natural diamonds are made from carbon-12).

1993 US company Intel markets the Pentium microprocessor chip for computers.

In 1892, German biologist Hans Driesch watched a fertilised sea urchin egg divide into two cells under a microscope. He then shook the tiny embryo until the two cells came apart. Each developed into a normal urchin larva. He had created identical twins, or clones.

The First Steps

In 1902, German scientist Hans Spemann took things a step further. He split a two-cell salamander embryo. Over the next four decades, Spemann investigated the possibilities of cloning. He predicted that one day it would be possible to create clones by transferring a nucleus from an adult cell into an egg cell from which the original nucleus had been removed. This means that instead of being a genetic blend of two parents, the newly created embryo would be an exact replica of the adult animal from which the original cell came.

Spemann's prediction became reality in two stages. In 1952, Americans Robert Briggs and Thomas J. King removed a cell from a northern leopard frog embryo and transferred it into an unfertilised frog egg cell from which the nucleus had been removed. The clone developed normally.

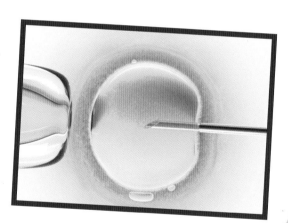

Timeline

1892 German biologist Hans Driesch creates cloned sea urchin larva

1902 German scientist Hans Spemann creates salamander clones

1952 Americans Robert Briggs and Thomas J. King clone a frog using a nucleus from an embryo cell

1958 Scientists at Oxford University clone a frog using a nucleus from an adult cell

1963 The word 'clone' first appears

1984 First mammal clone

1986 Dolly the sheep is cloned

← Genetic research continues in laboratories all over the world. In this false-colour magnified image, a pipette is used to inject DNA into an unfertilised egg.

1993 Japanese company Mazda announces plans to construct a fuel-efficient car using a Miller-cycle internal combustion engine.

1994 For the first time, more computers than TV sets are sold throughout the world.

1994 US scientists at Fermilab announce the discovery of the evasive subatomic particle called the top quark.

1994

1993 US astronomers Carolyn Shoemaker and David Levy discover a new comet, Shoemaker–Levy 9.

1994 A genetically modified tomato is marketed in the United States with the name 'Flavr Savr'.

1994 English mathematician Andrew Wiles offers a proof of Fermat's last theorem, a famous maths problem posed over 300 years earlier.

Cells are removed from a Dorset ewe (1a) and DNA replication starts (2a). An egg is removed from a blackface ewe (1b) and its nucleus is removed (2b). The nucleus from one of the Dorset ewe cells is fused with the

Dorset ewe   **Scottish blackface ewe**

1a   1b

2a   2b   **Nucleus removed**

3   **Early embryo**

egg (3). The cell divides to form an embryo (4), which is placed into a ewe (5). Dolly is identical to the nucleus donor (6).

4   **Surrogate mother**

Dorset lamb (Dolly)   5

6

Then, in 1958, scientists at Oxford University in England succeeded in performing a similar procedure, but this time using a nucleus from an adult cell. The fact that the donor cells were fully mature and thus separate from one another was important, because it proved that adult cells keep a full set of genetic material despite the fact that only part of it is expressed. British-born scientist John Burdon Haldane coined the term 'clone' in 1963. It comes from the Greek word for 'twig'.

Cloning Mammals

In 1977, a scientist at the University of Geneva in Switzerland caused a sensation when he claimed to have cloned three mice. Karl Illmensee claimed to have used much the same nuclear transfer techniques as those used to create the amphibian clones. Other scientists were incredulous because mammalian cells are much smaller, and nobody could understand how he had managed to manipulate them. Illmensee was never able to satisfy his critics, and in due course his claim came to be regarded as a fraud.

The first reliably documented mammal clone was produced in 1984 by a research group at Cambridge University in England led by Steen Willadsen. Willadsen and his colleagues cloned a sheep by transferring the

TIMELINE
1995–1998

1995 Russian cosmonaut Valeri Polyakov completes a record 438-day mission on the space station *Mir*.

1995 US geophysicists detect the rotation of the Earth's solid inner core through analysis of seismic waves.

1996 European scientists produce the first example of antimatter, antihydrogen.

KEY: 1995   1996

Astronomy and Maths

Biology and Medicine

Chemistry and Physics

Engineering and Invention

1995 US computer programmer James Gosling introduces the Java programming language.

1996 US astronomers find traces of what might be microscopic life in a meteorite that originated from Mars.

1996 Scottish biologist Ian Wilmut clones a sheep named Dolly.

Human Clones

Human clones already exist: identical twins are natural clones formed when an early embryo splits in half. But the artificial cloning of humans has stirred up a heated ethical debate. On one hand, the medical benefits could be enormous. They could have applications in the treatment of conditions such as Parkinson's disease and diabetes. On the other hand, the prospect of creating life to order or creating clones to replace loved ones remains disturbing to many people.

nucleus of an embryonic sheep cell into an empty egg. Two years later, Ian Wilmut began work in Edinburgh, Scotland. Wilmut was to become famous as the man who created 'Dolly the sheep'. Dolly went on to bear six lambs of her own in the normal way, but her health was poor. Since Dolly, many more mammals have been cloned. In 1997, Wilmut created Polly, a sheep cloned from foetal cells genetically altered to include a human gene. Other cloned animals include pigs, cattle, mice and a racehorse.

↑ This litter of cloned pigs was created in 2001 to help with medical research.

1997 US physicists led by Eric Cornell produce an atomic laser.

1997 US geneticist Huntington Willard assembles an artificial human chromosome that successfully replicates.

1998 US researchers grow human stem cells in the laboratory (stem cells may one day be used to treat cellular disorders).

1997

1998

1997 NASA probe *Mars Pathfinder* and its rover send back 16,500 images of the surface of Mars.

1998 The world's largest passenger terminal opens at Chek Lap Kok Airport in Hong Kong.

1998 After 15 years' work, an international project works out the genetic code for a whole animal – a tiny nematode worm.

Global Warming

Most people link the greenhouse effect with the phenomenon of global warming. But it is a fortuitous natural phenomenon that makes our planet habitable.

⟶⟩ Factory gases and car exhausts are leading contributors to global warming.

TIMELINE
1999–2002

KEY:

- Astronomy and Maths
- Biology and Medicine
- Chemistry and Physics
- Engineering and Invention

1999 Russian researchers create a new element, element 114.

2000 British inventor Matthew Allwork perfects a gyrostabilised camera that runs along tracks to televise sports events.

2000 NASA's space probe *Galileo* reveals that Jupiter's moon Io is highly volcanic.

1999

2000

1999 A much-feared 'millennium bug' fails to damage the world's computers on 31 December.

1999 According to the World Health Organization, AIDS becomes the main cause of death in Africa.

2000 Geneticists figure out the complete genome sequence of the fruit fly *Drosophila*.

One consequence of rising temperatures is the melting of the polar ice caps.

The greenhouse effect is nothing new. Earth has benefited from it for billions of years. The overall effect is an insulating one – the natural greenhouse effect keeps Earth's average temperature about 30 degrees higher than it would otherwise be.

Changes in Climate

During the early 20th century, scientists were aware that Earth's climate had previously undergone dramatic changes and that it was currently enjoying a period of relative warmth, called an interglacial period. Aware of the greenhouse role of carbon dioxide (CO_2), Swedish physical chemist Svante Arrhenius suspected that cooling events (ice ages) might have been caused by reduced levels of atmospheric CO_2. He calculated the amount of CO_2 released by human activities and realised that, over a prolonged period of time, such output could begin to have a reverse effect. In 1896, Arrhenius was the first to suggest that, instead of facing global cooling, the world might experience global warming as a result of industrial emissions. The idea was revived

Timeline

1827 Fourier describes the greenhouse effect

1896 Arrhenius publishes a theory of global warming linked to human-made emission of greenhouse gases

1939 Callendar observes a rise in both global temperatures and CO_2 levels

1979 First World Climate Conference

1985 First international conference on the greenhouse effect (Villach, Austria)

1988 United Nations sets up the Intergovernmental Panel on Climate Change (IPCC)

1998 The hottest year in the hottest decade in the hottest century of the millennium

2005 Kyoto Protocol comes into effect

2001 Surgeons in New York City use computers to operate on a woman in France.

2002 The Hubble Space Telescope is upgraded by a NASA mission.

2002 US chemists synthesise a compound of uranium and the rare gas neon.

2001

2002

2001 The Very Large Telescope (VLT) is completed at the Paranal Observatory in Chile.

2002 Researchers in the United States clone a domestic cat.

2002 Researchers at the University of New York produce a synthetic virus.

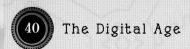

The Greenhouse Effect in Action

Some solar radiation is bounced straight out into space by gases in the atmosphere. But a lot passes through and hits Earth's surface. Some is absorbed and some is reflected. The reflected heat (albedo) takes the form of long-wave infrared radiation. Gas molecules in the atmosphere absorb the radiation and keep it from being lost into space. The gas particles begin to reradiate energy in all directions. About 30 per cent is radiated back down to Earth's surface.

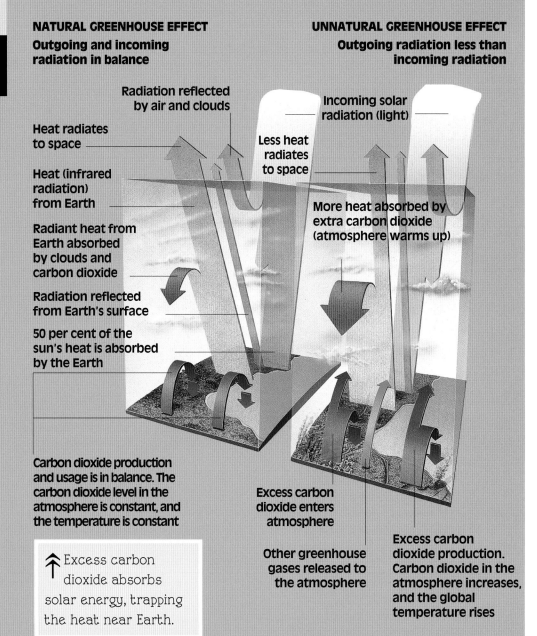

NATURAL GREENHOUSE EFFECT
Outgoing and incoming radiation in balance

UNNATURAL GREENHOUSE EFFECT
Outgoing radiation less than incoming radiation

Radiation reflected by air and clouds

Incoming solar radiation (light)

Heat radiates to space

Less heat radiates to space

Heat (infrared radiation) from Earth

Radiant heat from Earth absorbed by clouds and carbon dioxide

More heat absorbed by extra carbon dioxide (atmosphere warms up)

Radiation reflected from Earth's surface

50 per cent of the sun's heat is absorbed by the Earth

Carbon dioxide production and usage is in balance. The carbon dioxide level in the atmosphere is constant, and the temperature is constant

Excess carbon dioxide enters atmosphere

Other greenhouse gases released to the atmosphere

Excess carbon dioxide production. Carbon dioxide in the atmosphere increases, and the global temperature rises

↑ Excess carbon dioxide absorbs solar energy, trapping the heat near Earth.

TIMELINE
2003–2006

KEY:

- Astronomy and Maths
- Biology and Medicine
- Chemistry and Physics
- Engineering and Invention

2003

2004

2003 NASA's Space Shuttle *Columbia* is destroyed as it re-enters Earth's atmosphere, killing all of the crew.

2004 US physicists announce a helium-based 'supersolid' that flows through another material without friction.

2003 An outbreak of severe acute respiratory syndrome (SARS) in Asia spreads worldwide.

2004 Palaeontologists on Flores Island, Indonesia, discover the remains of a 90-centimetre (3-ft) tall hominid, *Homo floresiensis*.

2005 US geophysicists discover that lightning flashes produce bursts of X-rays.

in 1939 by English scientist Guy Stewart Callendar. He suggested that increases in temperatures and CO_2 levels were linked. From then on, the idea refused to go away.

Global Warming

In the 1960s, it became possible to measure atmospheric carbon dioxide levels accurately, and it became clear they were rising rapidly. Climate models began to take account of variables such as ocean absorption and clouds. The year 1988 marked a turning point. Globally, it was the hottest year on record (there have been many hotter ones since), and it was the year that public awareness of global warming took off.

Between 1890 and 1990, the amount of CO_2 in the atmosphere rose by a quarter from 280 to 345 parts per million by volume. By the end of the 20th century, scientists reached a consensus that the world is warming and that the trend is the result of human activities. In 1997, 84 nations agreed to curb emissions by signing the Kyoto Protocol. The United States did not sign but pledged to reduce emissions. Later global climate summits, including in 2009 in Copenhagen, Denmark, and in 2014 in Lima, Peru, failed to make many significant advances.

↓ Most scientists accept that global warming is causing more frequent droughts. There are still a few opponents, however, who argue that global warming is part of a natural cycle.

2005 A projectile fired from a NASA probe collides with Comet Tempel 1, allowing scientists to study the plume of icy debris thrown up by the impact.

2005 The Genographic Project is set up to map the history of human migration by tracing DNA.

2006 Scientists in Canada discover the fossil of a 'missing link' between fish and four-legged vertebrates.

2005

2006

2005 NASA grounds its shuttle fleet indefinitely after problems with heat-shield tiles on *Discovery*.

2006 NASA launches the probe *New Horizons* on a nine-year voyage to Pluto.

2006 Boeing launches the world's largest aeroplane, the 747 Large Cargo Freighter (known as the Dreamlifter).

The World Wide Web

The dream of a universal information database was realised in 1990 with the launch of the World Wide Web. Users have access to a vast amount of data instantly.

→ Internet servers contain huge amounts of information in highly secure environments.

TIMELINE
2007–2010

KEY:

- Astronomy and Maths
- Biology and Medicine
- Chemistry and Physics
- Engineering and Invention

2007 Scientists in the United States power a light bulb with 'wireless' electricity.

2007 US geneticist J. Craig Venter publishes his entire genetic sequence, the first of a single person.

2008 India launches its first lunar spacecraft.

2007

2008

2007 US company Apple markets the iPhone, a multimedia smartphone with a touchscreen.

2008 The Large Hadron Collider is switched on at the European Organization for Nuclear Research (CERN). Nine days later, it is switched off again because of a fault.

The World Wide Web uses telephone lines or radio waves to link computers into a global network. The web allows computer users to gain immediate access to billions of pages of documents as well as video, films and music. English computer scientist Tim Berners-Lee devised the web in 1990.

Early Computer Connections

Computer links had existed since the 1970s. In 1981, the City University of New York launched BITNET (the 'BIT' standing for 'because it's time'). EUNET followed in 1982. These networks were limited by the difficulty of generating information on one computer in a form that could be read by other computers. The problem was solved within each network, but one network was unable to communicate with computers belonging to another.

As early as 1974, computer scientists had devised a system called a transmission control protocol/internet protocol (TCP/IP) to allow computers to send data between networks. Henceforth, networks could be

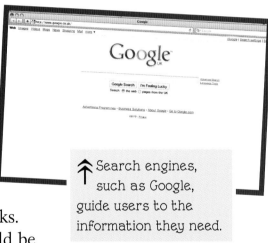

↑ Search engines, such as Google, guide users to the information they need.

Timeline

1980 Tim Berners-Lee envisages the World Wide Web

1981 BITNET launched

1982 EUNET launched; Internet born

1984 EARN launched; domain names introduced; JANET launched

1985 NSFNET launched

1990 Tim Berners-Lee names the World Wide Web

1991 NSFNET opened to the public; the web is released to the public

1992 'Information superhighway project'

1993 Mosaic X, the first web browser, is introduced

1993 World Wide Web is certified by CERN as being in the public domain

---

2009 Japanese scientists report that decomposing plastics are creating a 'toxic soup' in the oceans.

2010 US geneticist Craig Venter creates the first artificial life form, a new bacterium.

2010 The explosion of the Deepwater Horizon oil platform in the Gulf of Mexico causes the worst marine environmental disaster in US history.

2009 — 2010

2009 The Human Genome Organisation reports that DNA studies suggest that Asia was populated in a single migration from the south.

2010 Apple launches the iPad, a tablet computer operated by a touchscreen.

2010 Japan launches IKAROS, a probe headed to Venus and the Sun powered for the first time by solar-sail technology.

Domain Name Servers

To receive messages, each host has a unique address. In 1984, this system introduced domain name servers. A domain name server stores lists of domain names and can route requests accordingly. Domain names include http:// (hypertext transfer protocol), www (World Wide Web), ac (academic), edu (education), com (commercial) and gov (government), as well as national identifiers, such as uk (United Kingdom), de (Germany), fr (France) and nl (Netherlands).

linked: the Internet had been born, and with it, email. A computer linked to a network is called a host, and email proved so popular that, by 1984, there were more than 1,000 hosts generating a high volume of traffic.

Communication Grows

The Internet received a further boost in 1984 when the British government backed JANET (Joint Academic Network) to serve British universities. In 1985, the US National Science Foundation set up NSFNET to extend Internet use to authorised persons on every American campus. In 1988, NSFNET upgraded the network capacity from 56,000 to 1.544 million bytes per second. Following the opening of NSFNET, the number of Internet users grew from about 5,000 in 1986 to 28,000 in 1987, although only people in research or education could access the network. In 1991, NSFNET allowed access to private computers. In 1992, Senator Al Gore introduced the High-Performance Computing Act, nicknamed the 'information superhighway project'.

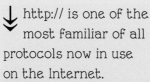

↓ http:// is one of the most familiar of all protocols now in use on the Internet.

TIMELINE
2011-2014

KEY:

Astronomy and Maths

Biology and Medicine

Chemistry and Physics

Engineering and Invention

2011 Swedish surgeons transplant the world's first synthetic organ, a windpipe.

2011 China's Three Gorges Dam, the largest power plant in history, becomes fully operational.

2012 The Mars Science Laboratory, or Curiosity, explores the Red Planet.

2011

2012

2011 *Atlantis* flies on the 135th – and final – mission of the Space Shuttle programme.

2011 The world's first commercial spaceport opens in the United States.

2012 The first quad-core smartphones and pads are released, offering a significant increase in processing power.

The World Wide Web

Since 1980, English scientist Tim Berners-Lee had been a software developer at the European Organization for Nuclear Research (CERN) in Switzerland. He was looking for a way to allow communication between physicists in different countries using different computer systems. By 1991, he had written a program to achieve this; he named it the World Wide Web.

Berners-Lee released the program to CERN workers, and in August 1991, the program was published on the Internet, free for anyone. The World Wide Web was born – but it grew slowly. By the end of 1993, there were only about 150 sites. Then, in 1993, American Marc Andreessen of the National Center for Supercomputing Applications released the first browser, Mosaic X (later renamed Netscape). A browser means that, instead of typing in the address of a required document, the user clicks on a hypertext link indicated by words in a different colour. Where the Internet linked computers, the World Wide Web linked documents. Today, there are probably more than 180 million websites and over 4.3 billion web pages.

↑ Broadband and wireless systems mean that rapid access to the Internet can be achieved with portable devices from virtually anywhere in the world.

2013 China overtakes the United States as the world's leading nation for scientific research.

2013 The space camera Gaia is launched to map a billion stars in the Milky Way.

2014 Launched in 2004, the probe Rosetta lands on Comet 67P.

2013

2014

2013 The European Union approves the first gene therapy in the West, Glybera.

2014 Google launch Google Glass, an augmented reality head-mounted display offering hands-free access to the Internet.

2014 A Virgin Galactic spacecraft crashes in the United States, in a blow to plans for commercial space transport.

Glossary

atom The smallest unit into which matter can be divided and still retain its chemical identity.

black smoker A hole on the seabed that releases superheated water containing many minerals.

chromosome A thread-like structure in the nucleus of a living cell that carries genetic information.

crystallography The branch of science concerned with the structure of crystals.

diffraction Spreading a beam of light by passing it through a narrow gap or across an edge.

DNA (deoxyribonucleic acid) A chemical substance that, with proteins, makes up the chromosomes found in the nuclei of most cells; the basis of genetic inheritance in most living organisms.

echolocation A system for locating objects by reflecting sound off them.

electron A negatively charged subatomic particle.

gene The basic unit of inheritance that influences a characteristic of a living organism.

ion An atom or molecule that has acquired an electrical charge.

isotopes Forms of an element that share the same number of protons but different numbers of neutrons.

laser (light amplification by stimulated emission of radiation) A device that produces an intense beam of light that is monochromatic (all of the same wavelength) and coherent (all the light waves are synchronised).

nucleotide A basic unit of packaging of DNA in a chromosome, in which a sugar molecule is linked to one or more phosphate groups.

nucleus, atomic (pl nuclei) The positively charged dense region at the centre of an atom, composed of protons and neutrons.

neutron A subatomic particle that has no electrical charge and is found in the atomic nucleus.

payload The part of a cargo that earns revenue.

proton A positively charged subatomic particle in the atomic nucleus.

pulsar A rapidly rotating neutron star that emits regular pulses of radio waves.

quark A subatomic particle carrying a tiny electrical charge.

radioactivity The emission of particles or radiation by atomic nuclei.

subatomic particle Any particle that is smaller than an atom.

superconductor A substance that shows no resistance to the passage of electrical current (usually at very low temperatures).

synthesise To chemically form a compound from simpler elements.

vaccine A preparation containing viruses or other microorganisms introduced (often by injection) into the body to stimulate the formation of antibodies to build up immunity against infectious disease.

Further Reading

Books

Barber, Nicola. *Cloning and Genetic Engineering* (Both Sides of the Story). Franklin Watts, 2014.

Chorlton, Windsor. *The Invention of the Silicon Chip: A Revolution in Daily Life* (Point of Impact). Heinemann Library, 2002.

Clements, Gillian. *The First Moon Landing* (Great Events). Franklin Watts, 2014.

Goldsmith, Mike, and Tom Jackson. *Computer* (Eyewitness Books). DL Publishing, 2011.

Green, Dan. *Technology: A Bite-Sized World* (Basher Science). Kingfisher, 2012.

Harvey, Damian. *Tim Berners-Lee* (History Heroes). Franklin Watts, 2014.

Martin, Claudia. *Tim Berners-Lee: Creator of the Web* (Inspirational Lives). Wayland, 2015.

Parker, Steve. *Climate* (Changes In). QED Publishing, 2009.

Vaughn, Jenny. *Who Discovered DNA?* (Breakthroughs in Science and Technology). Arcturus Publishing, 2010.

Yates, Vicki. *Communication* (Then and Now). Heinemann Educational, 2007.

Websites

inventors.about.com/library/ blcoindex.htm
About.com timeline of milestones in computer history.

www.computersciencelab.com/ ComputerHistory/History.htm
Computer Science Lab illustrated history of computers.

spaceflight.nasa.gov/history/ apollo/
NASA history of the Apollo programme.

science.howstuffworks.com/ space-shuttle.htm
How Stuff Works pages on the Space Shuttle.

www.scienceclarified.com/ Ci-Co/Clone-and-Cloning.html
Science Clarified pages about the history of cloning.

Index